A Cookbook

For Caregivers

A Cookbook

For Caregivers

A caregiver's guide to cooking healthy meals that support
brain health in seniors, children
and even yourself.

*An entire week of recipes, including everything you need
with a grocery list, recommended utensils and cooking tools*

Janet Laidler

www.janetlaidler.com

ISBN 13: 978-0692738498

ISBN 10: 0692738495

Acknowledgements

This book is dedicated to my father and mother, James and Carolynn Laidler, who gave their time and spent their lives taking care of others.

I also want to thank the following people:

Dr. Robert Milne; his guidance and advice on nutrition. He has helped me stay healthy and feel great throughout the past 20 years.

Monica Deeter, Bruce Economou and Kimberly Laidler, for their editing advice.

Dr. Martin Flynn, a physician involved in the practice of age management who lives the healthy lifestyle he preaches to others.

Prologue

As a physician involved in healthy aging, this book resonates with me on a number of levels.

First, Janet is like all caretakers who accept this sacred responsibility: unsung and often invisible, but so strong in maintaining their quiet dignity and that of their dependents. So, she wrote a book with the same gentle spirit; it's more of a conversation than an instruction manual.

Then, there's the practical. This is a book that's simple and notes some ease in our daily effort. When we "Make Health A Game!", there will always be time to add new information and improve overall nutrition but it's so important to start with the fundamentals. Janet allows you to relax a bit and let her words be your guide. May you and your loved ones find comfort and good food in this.

Martin Flynn MD   Venice, CA

Note to the Reader

This is not your average cookbook. It is more than just recipes. It is a step-by-step guide to managing time for meal planning, shopping, preparation and serving healthy, delicious meals. I developed it based on the recommendations from the research and resources listed in the back of this book, focusing on phytonutrients for anti-aging, protein rotation, and plain old fashioned taste! And, it extends beyond seniors.

We know our diet affects our wellbeing at any age. But, as a personal chef, I have found that no matter our age, we still want to eat the food we grew up with whether it is good for us or not. The focus of this book is to make it easy for caregivers to provide both taste and foods that enhance brain health.

Even working parents with children and teens, young professionals or grad students with little time on their hands will appreciate the time saving methods for preparing fresh grocery-to-table meals. But this book makes it easier than a traditional cookbook.

Yet, I will acknowledge, everyone wants to eat their comfort food. So, I have taken those foods and applied what I have learned through research over the years, and put a healthy twist on them to promote brain health. The book presents fresh combinations of food intended to help the absorption of nutrients through the blood-brain barrier in a variety of the brain's lobes.

The book provides a week's worth of meals, a list of the kitchen tools needed, and a grocery list. Every meal's preparation is timed out with step-by-step instructions. You go to the store only once, and by the end of the week, all of the food is used…no waste. This way, everything is fresh. It tastes better, and it is healthier. Why wouldn't anyone want to buy it for just that reason?

The impetus for writing this book was for my own parent's caregiver. I was living in Las Vegas and visiting my parents in Michigan from time-to-time. I cooked the food for them that I made for myself. I also rotated the proteins so that brain function would be optimal for their medication absorption. There was a noticeable improvement in their attentiveness and energy by the end of my visit. I talked to their doctor and the nurse at the home care agency about getting them healthier meals, explaining that I could see how the food I prepared had had a positive effect on them. They both told me there are no guides or books for caregivers about cooking for home care or seniors, just regular cookbooks.

They were right. I searched the Internet and bookstores, and could find nothing that addressed the needs of caregivers for recipes and meal planning, let alone guides for shopping or time management. And certainly nothing about the importance of protein rotation and the planning that alone requires. This was not acceptable to me…so I wrote the book myself. This book fills that void.

How to use this Book

-Pull out the grocery list and cross out all of the items you already have in your kitchen and pantry. Then buy the items that you did not cross out. Buy organic produce if you can get it. The kind of juice or cereal on the list is just a suggestion. Keep cereal high fiber based and avoid corn syrup in both.

-Nuts are full of nutrition, but they are always listed as optional as some seniors have difficulty chewing and swallowing nuts. This is something you will have to decide. If not sure, discuss with your doctor or visiting nurse. If you choose to serve nuts, make sure they are shelled!!

-Pull out the kitchen tools list and do the same thing, cross out what you already have in the kitchen. You may not have to buy the remaining items if you know how to use another items in its place. This is up to you. But having the right tool will make everything easy and fast.

-Every recipe is written for 2 servings, two people. Some days more food is made on purpose to have leftovers for the next day's menu. If you have more in your household to cook for, you will want to adjust the recipes, thus change the amounts on your grocery list. For example, if you have 4 people instead, double everything. If you are cooking for one, cut everything in half.

-When you return from the grocery, remove any packaging (discard packaging) and labels from all produce put them in a clean sink filled with water and ¼ cup of apple cider vinegar. Cleaning all of your produce right away with the vinegar based solution will not only reduce prep time, but will keep them fresh.

-Put them into fresh plastic bags or wrap in paper towels and put them into the refrigerator to store until use. Cut the bananas into four pieces and put them in a plastic bag and store in the freezer. Frozen bananas give smoothies a nice consistency.

-You may want to make all of the salad dressings and sauces first thing to save time when cooking. But if you don't, do not worry as they only take a few minutes to make.

-Try to organize at the beginning of each day by putting the mealtime on the weekly menu chart. It is always nice to anticipate when meals are being served.

-Always start your meal preparation by setting the table, gathering the tools and ingredients you need. This way, when you are ready to serve, everything will be in its place for you to put the food on the table. You may notice I include a box of facial tissue on the table. Some people, like my father, get a runny nose while eating and it's handy for them.

-I am going to assume that everyone knows how to make coffee or tea. If not, each coffeemaker is different, and comes with instructions specific to it, or you can simply ask a friend to show you how to use it, and help you decide what kind of coffee to buy.

Week's Menu Chart

DAY	BREAKFAST	LUNCH	SNACKS	DINNER
1	FRUIT SMOOTHIE OAT PANCAKES MAPLE SYRUP	BROCCOLI SOUP ½ TURKEY AVOCADO, TOMATO & LETTUCE SANDWICH	DRIED FRUIT NUTS	SALMON ROASTED BRUSSEL SPROUTS YAM CUPCAKE
2	FRUIT SMOOTHIE EGG TOAST JAM	TUNA MELT PEACHES	RED GRAPES	POT ROAST MASHED POTATOES BROCCOLI ICE CREAM
3	OATMEAL RAISINS FLAXSEED GRAPE JUICE	NAVY BEAN SOUP CRACKERS	DRIED FRUIT OR FRUIT POPSICLE	MOM'S FAVORITE SALAD ROSEMARY CHICKEN THIGHS GREEN BEANS WITH RICE CUPCAKE
4	RAISIN BRAN RICE MILK FLAXSEED BERRIES APRICOT NECTAR	CHOPPED GREENS SALMON SALAD SANDWICH	OATMEAL COOKIES	PICO DE GALLO BEEF TACOS GUACAMOLE CHIPS & SALSA ICE CREAM
5	OATMEAL RICE MILK FLAXSEED BERRIES JUICE	ROMAINE SALAD W/AVOCADO GRILLED HAM AND CHEESE SANDWICH	DRIED FRUIT	MOM'S FAVORITE SALAD BONELESS PORK CHOPS CAULIFLOWER FRUIT PIE
6	CEREAL RICE MILK BERRIES FLAXSEED JUICE	CHOPPED GREENS ½ CHICKEN SALAD SANDWICH	RED GRAPES	PAN SEARED FISH ROASTED POTATOES AND BROCCOLI CUPCAKE
7	FRUIT SMOOTHIE OATMEAL W/ RICE MILK	FRITATA TOAST FRUIT	OATMEAL COOKIES	MOM'S FAVORITE SALAD CHEESE BURGER LEFT OVER VEGETABLES DESSERT

**Check these items with what you already have.
Cross out what you have and buy the rest.**

Produce
Broccoli 3 crowns
Cilantro, I bunch
Romaine lettuce 1 head
Green leaf lettuce, 1 head
Iceberg lettuce, 1 head
Celery
Carrot, 4
Kale, 1 bunch lacinato
Collard Greens, 1 bunch
Yellow pepper, 1
Cauliflower (one head)
Brussel sprouts 10-12
Green beans, dozen
1 pint container cherry tomatoes
3 cucumbers
3 avocados
1 tomato – medium size
1 medium sweet onions
2 small brown onions
1 small red onion
1 portobello mushroom
1 yams
1 large russet potato
Pint blueberries
Pint raspberries
3 bananas
3 lemons
3 limes
4 small redskin potatoes
Red grapes

Meat
¾ lb. of cod, snapper, or any white fish
1 ¼ lb. salmon
2/3 lb. 15% fat ground beef
6 chicken thighs, boneless, but with skin
1 package ham, nitrate free, uncured
1 lb. roast beef, lean chuck roast or tri tip
1/4 lb turkey lunchmeat (uncured , nitrate free)
3-4 thin cut pork chops, boneless

Bread
1 loaf multigrain, high fiber bread
Hamburger buns, whole grain
Corn tortillas

Dairy
1 small bag grated, r-best free, cheddar cheese
Grated parmesan cheese
1/2 lb. butter
2 32 oz. cartons of rice milk
1 dozen eggs
2 small vanilla yogurt
Whipped cream
Ice cream (you choose the flavor)

General grocery
Mustard
Ground coffee
Extra virgin olive oil
1 bottle white wine vinegar
Raw, unfiltered honey
Pure maple syrup
32 oz. box chicken broth
32 oz. container vegetable stock
1 jar mayonnaise (at least 15 oz.)
1 can garbanzo beans
White cane sugar
1 box golden brown sugar
1 16 oz. can navy beans
1 small can coconut milk
Jar of sliced dill chips
ketchup
I bag oat flour
Cupcake baking cups
Cheez it (or favorite snack cracker)
Favorite cracker for soup
Can of chicken breast
2- 5 oz cans of tuna
One 3-pack of peaches in water
(cup of fruit snacks)
1 small jar minced garlic

**Check these items with what you already have.
Cross out what you have and buy the rest.**

<u>Bulk</u>

Dried cranberries (sulfate free)
Dried cherries (organic or sulfate free)
1 cup raisins
Walnuts, pecans or pistachios necessary
1 small bag of brown rice (1 cup)
Flaxseed, about ½ cup
2 cups rolled oats
Approx. 1 cup semi-sweet or dark
chocolate chips

<u>Drinks</u>

Cranberry juice (juice based)
Any tea of choice
Other juice of choice such as apricot
nectar
If soda is a choice, consider buying a
stevia or natural sweetener based one.
Stay away from corn syrup based sodas

<u>Spices</u>

Baking powder
Baking soda
Bay leaf
cinnamon
Cream of tartar
dill
ground black pepper
Italian herbs
Kosher sea salt
Nutmeg
onion powder
oregano
paprika
rosemary
Thyme
Vanilla extract

Kitchen Tool List

These are very typical kitchen items that you probably already have in your kitchen. Everything you will use for the entire week is listed below. The exact size is not necessary, but it will make it easier for you. If you do not have a smaller pot/pan, you can use the larger one instead. You just cannot substitute a small pan for a large one.

Recommended:
- Check all utensils to see if they easy to grip and hold.
- Check all of your knives to ensure they are sharp. Sharpen them if dull.
- You should have at least 4 place settings, sets of dishes, and silverware.
- Cups with big handles and glasses with ridges so they are easy to hold.
- Cutting board should be large, easy to pick up and clean. Two boards, one for meat, and one for vegetables is ideal, but not necessary if you clean it well.

10 to 12 oz. glass jar with a lid.
1 ½ quart sauce pan with lid medium)
1 qt. saucepan (small)
2 qt. saucepan with lid (large)
2.5 qt. crockpot, or larger
Two 1 cup measuring cups
One 2 cup measuring cup
9x13 glass baking pan
Aluminum foil
Baking sheet
Metal baking pan, 9" x 13"
Blender
Knife for chopping, large chef style
Knife for slicing/cutting
Small paring knife
Knife serrated, for bread
Can opener
Cheese grater
Citrus juicer

Cutting board
Large cooking fork
Small and large frying pan with lids
Set of mixing bowls, sm, med, lg
Large spoon for cooking
Large spoons or salad tongs
One small rubber spatula
One regular rubber spatula
Oven mitts
Paper towels
Potato masher
Potato peeler
Salad tongs for tossing
Set of measuring spoons
Large slotted spoon
Small fork
Soup ladle
Large heat resistant spatula
Toaster
Tongs for cooking and serving

<u>Day One</u>

Oat Pancakes with Berries

Day One

First Thing!

✓ Medications are best taken at least 45 minutes before meals. If the prescription specifies they are to be taken with food, then serve them with the meal instead.

Menu

Breakfast	Lunch	Dinner*
Fruit Smoothie Oat Pancakes Berries Juice	Broccoli Soup ½ Turkey Sandwich with avocado, lettuce & tomato	Pan seared Salmon Roasted Brussel Sprouts Yam *Cupcake
Afternoon Snack: Dried Fruit and/or Nuts		

*Cupcake and frosting recipe is in the recipe section in the back of the book.

Breakfast

Prep time: 10 minutes

Place on the table
A knife, fork, glass of water, napkin, facial tissue.

Ingredients	Tools
1 kale leaf ½ cup blueberries ½ cup raspberries 1 frozen banana 2 teaspoon flaxseed ½ cup yogurt 1 cup rice milk honey to taste	measuring cup cutting board blender large glass

When you have everything you need,

1) Take the lid off of the blender. Tear the kale leaves in half and put them along with the blueberries, raspberries, banana, flaxseed, rice milk and yogurt in the blender. Add a small dab of honey for sweetness if desired.
2) Place the lid back on the blender, turn on to lowest speed until the ingredients are mixed together.

3) Turn it up to the next highest speed and blend for 10 seconds. Then to the next highest for 10 seconds and continue blending until smooth and foamy.
4) Turn it off. Take the lid off, pour it into a glass and serve!

Ingredients
1 tbsp. flaxseed
3/4 cup rice milk
1/2 cup oat flour
1/2 cup oatmeal
1/2 teaspoon baking powder
dash cinnamon
dash salt
½ teaspoon vanilla
1 tablespoon olive oil
2 eggs
1 tablespoon olive oil
berries

Tools
small measuring cup
blender
measuring cup
spoon
griddle or frying pan
small rubber spatula
spatula for fry pan

Fruit Smoothie   *For Oatmeal Pancakes*

Wash out the blender and place it aside to dry while you get the pancakes ready. When you have everything together,

1) Put the flour, oatmeal, baking powder, salt, one tablespoon of olive oil, egg, rice milk and flaxseed in the blender.
2) Put the lid on the blender and push the button for the lowest speed. Blend until smooth and then turn it up to medium high speed and puree.
3) You may have to remove the lid, take the small rubber spatula, scrape the sides of the blender and push the mixture to the bottom and blend again.
4) Turn off the blender remove the carafe from the unit.
5) Put the pan/griddle on the stove over a medium high heat, Add the remaining olive oil to the pan.
6) Let it heat for about 30 seconds.
7) Pour some batter into the pan, making 2 to 3 inch sized circle cakes.

8) Watch for the cakes to bubble on top, and the bubbles pop open. If you chose to add berries, drop a few into each oatcake now or serve them separately fresh on the plate (as pictured one page 1).
9) Next, with the spatula, flip them over. Cook for another minute.
10) Put 2 to 3 cakes on a plate. If you chose to have the fruit fresh, serve it on the plate with the cakes and maple syrup.
11) Turn off the stove!

Any leftover batter can be stored in a closed container in the refrigerator for up to a week to reuse. **Then clean up your dishes, wipe down the table and cooking areas.**

<u>Lunch</u>

Prep time: about 30 minutes

✓ Medications are best taken at least 45 minutes before meals. If the prescription specifies they are to be taken with food, then serve them with the meal instead.

> ### <u>Place on the table</u>
> A soup spoon, glass of water, napkin and facial tissue.

Start lunch by getting the following things together:

<u>Ingredients</u>	<u>Tools</u>
1/2 cup chopped brown onion	comfortable knife to chop with
1/2 of a yellow pepper	cutting board
½ stalk celery	large saucepan with lid
½ cup carrot	large spoon
1 large leaf dark kale	blender
2 cups fresh broccoli – chopped	small rubber spatula
sprig of cilantro	oven mitts
3 tablespoons olive oil	2 soup bowls
1/2 teaspoon minced garlic	
1 teaspoon salt,	
¼ teaspoon pepper	
32 ounce box of vegetable broth	
Water	
½ of a lemon	
1/2 cup coconut milk	
grated cheddar cheese	
optional: ½ avocado	

Day One

Once you have everything together,

1) Cut the onion, celery, carrot, pepper, kale and broccoli into chunks. Put them aside for a moment.
2) Put the saucepan on the stove; add the olive oil.
3) Turn the heat on medium high under the saucepan for about a minute. Add all of the vegetables and stir them until they are coated with oil.
4) Continue to cook, while stirring occasionally, for about 5 minutes.
5) Pour vegetable stock into the sauce pan and stir. Bring it to a boil,
6) Add the garlic, cilantro, salt and pepper. Bring it to a boil.
7) Once boiling, stir well and partially cover and cook over medium to low heat, keeping it at a slow, low boil for approximately 25 minutes or until all ingredients are soft. You should easily cut through the broccoli with the side of a fork. If the vegetable are not soft, keep slow boiling them until they are.

While the soup is cooking, you can prepare the sandwich.

You will need to get the following items:

Ingredients	Tools
2 slices bread	knife for slicing
2 slices of turkey	table knife
tomato	cutting board
avocado	small plate
leaf lettuce	
mayonnaise	

1) Start by putting the tomato on the cutting board and holding it with one hand, while you have the knife in the other. Place the knife on the tomato and slice off about a ¼ piece.
2) Place the bread on the cutting board. With the table knife, spread each side with mayonnaise
3) Take an avocado in one hand and with the knife, cut off ¼ of it and pull off the peel. Then separate it from the pit. If it doesn't come off easy, you can just scrape it and spread it on the bread, because that is where you are putting the avocado anyway!
4) Put two slices of turkey on the other piece of bread, place the tomato and lettuce on top of it.
5) Put the two pieces together and slice it in half.
6) Place ½ sandwiches on each plate.

<u>Day One</u>

Turkey Sandwich with Tomato, and Avocado

Now you can do the final prep and serve for the broccoli soup.

1) With oven mitts on, remove from heat and turn off the stove. Take a fork and stick the vegetable to make sure they are soft. If they are, let the soup cool for a few minutes.
2) Once cooled down, with oven mitts on, pour everything from the pot into the blender.
3) Add the coconut milk and squeeze in the lemon.
4) Put the lid on the blender and hit pulse until everything almost smooth but there are still a few small chunks in the soup for texture.
5) If it is too thick, you can add water or more vegetable broth to desired consistency and creaminess.
6) Pour directly from the blender into the bowl and garnish with grated cheddar cheese and /or avocado chunks. Garnish with cilantro and avocado. (See picture on next page.)
7) Place the bowl on the plate next to the sandwich and you are ready to eat!
8) Don't forget to serve tea, juice, or coffee with lunch as desired.

Remember to put away leftovers and clean up. You will be glad you did!

Broccoli Soup with Cheddar Toasts

<u>Afternoon Snack</u>

Put some dried fruit, such as apricots, cherries, or pineapple in a small bowl so they can snack if they want to. Add nuts only if they are able to chew them.

<u>Dinner</u>

Prep time: 45 minutes

✓ Medications are best taken at least 45 minutes before meals. If the prescription specifies they are to be taken with food, then serve them with the meal instead.

> ### <u>Place on the table</u>
> A knife, fork, glass of water, napkin and facial tissue.

Day One

Begin by washing your hands, then making the yams and Brussel sprouts. Get the following items:

Ingredients	Tools
Ingredients	**Tools**
1 yam	paring knife
butter	cutting board
10-12 brussel sprouts	an oven mitt
olive oil	metal baking pan
salt	

1) Preheat the oven to 400 degrees.
2) Wash the yams, and place them in the oven, directly on the oven rack.
3) With your knife, on the cutting board, take each sprout and trim off the stalk base and cut the sprout in half.
4) Once all are cut, place them in the pan (along with any leaves that have fallen off the sprouts as well) and coat them with olive oil...you can toss them with your hands.
5) Lightly salt them, and place them in the oven.
6) Set the timer for 40 minutes.

You get a little break since you don't have to start to get these together until 20 minutes before dinner:

Ingredients	Tools
Ingredients	**Tools**
1 ¼ lb. of salmon	measuring spoons
or 3 pieces about 5 oz. each	large frying pan with a lid
2 tablespoons olive oil	spatula
1 tablespoon dill weed	oven mitt
¼ teaspoon onion powder	2 dinner plates
¼ teaspoon paprika	
1/2 of a lemon	
honey	
tartar sauce	

Note: If you haven't done so, you can make it the tartar sauce now. The recipe is on page 55. When you are ready,

1) Rinse the salmon with cold water and pat dry between 2 paper towels
2) With the pan on the stove; add the olive oil, the dill weed, paprika and onion powder.

Salmon with Brussel Sprouts and Yams

3) Take the ½ lemon, and with the grater, grate about a tablespoon of lemon rind into the pan and with the edge of the spatula, mix everything together in the pan and spread evenly.
4) Turn the heat on medium high, and heat the ingredients until you see them begin to slightly sizzle.
5) Sporadically drizzle in about a teaspoon of honey and place the fish, skin side up, in the pan, letting it sear for about a minute.
6) Turn the heat down to medium and put the lid on the pan. Let it cook for about another 5 minutes.
7) Then, with an oven mitt on, remove the lid, and using the spatula, remove the skin from the fish, then flip the fish over in the pan.
8) Place the lid back on the pan and turn the heat on low. Continue to cook the fish for another 2 minutes then turn off the heat and remove from the burner and let it sit, with the lid on, until you are ready to serve.
9) When the 60 minutes are up, take the yams out of the oven and turn off the oven. Place them directly onto the plate, but give them a minute to cool down.

10) Take the lid of the frying pan, and with your spatula, flip the fish over onto to the plates with the seared/crusted side up.

11) Then, put the yams on the plate, make a small cut in the top to open the crust and add butter and salt to taste.

12) Serve with tartare sauce.

13) You are ready for a great meal!

Tonight's dessert is a cupcake. You don't have to serve it right away, you can clean up the dinner dishes, put everything away, and them sit down and relax with a sweet treat as a nice ending to the day.

Banana Cupcakes with Buttercream Frosting
One each topped with Blackberry, Raspberry and Lime Zest

<u>Day Two</u>

First Thing!

✓ Medications are best taken at least 45 minutes before meals. If the prescription specifies they are to be taken with food, then serve them with the meal instead.

<u>Menu</u>

<u>Breakfast</u>	<u>Lunch</u>	<u>Dinner</u>
Fruit Smoothie **An Egg on** **Whole Grain Toast** **Jam**	**Tuna Melt** **Peaches**	**Pot Roast** **Mashed Potatoes** **Broccoli** **Ice Cream**
<u>**Afternoon Snack:**</u> **Dried Fruit**		

Alert! Dinner prep has to begin in the morning as you are using the slow cooker. You can do it either before or after breakfast, whichever works out better for you.

*To cook the roast the traditional way in the oven, see recipe for "Dad's Favorite: Pot Roast" in the back on page 56. The prep timing will be different.

<u>Breakfast</u>

Prep time: 5 minutes

> ### <u>Place on the table</u>
> A knife, fork, jam, juice glass, glass of water, napkin, facial tissue.

Start with the smoothie. You will need the following items:

<u>Ingredients</u>	<u>Tools</u>
1/2 kale leaf	**measuring cup**
1/4 cup blueberries	**cutting board**
1/4 cup raspberries	**blender**
2 pieces of frozen banana	**water glass**
1 teaspoon flaxseed	
½ cup vanilla yogurt	
½ cup rice milk	

5) Take the lid off of the blender. Tear the kale into pieces.
6) Put in kale, blueberries, raspberries, banana, flaxseed, and yogurt and rice milk.

7) Place the lid back on the blender and turn on to lowest speed until the ingredients are mixed together.
8) Turn it up to the next highest speed, blend for 5 seconds, then to the next highest for 10 seconds and then to the highest speed until smooth and creamy.
9) Turn it off. Take the lid off, and pour it into a glass and serve!

Now you can make toast and a fried egg.

Fried Egg and Toast

Ingredients	Tools
one egg	spatula
1 teaspoon olive oil	non-stick fry pan
bread & butter	toaster
salt & pepper	dinner plate

1) Put the bread in the toaster and start to toast.
2) Put the pan on the stove, add the olive oil and turn the heat on medium.
3) Let it heat up until the oil begins to slightly sizzle.
4) Crack the egg into the pan and let it cook until it turns white and there is no more clear gel.
5) Take the spatula and wiggle it under the egg, flip it over. Let it cook for about 30 seconds.

6) Again using your spatula, carefully wiggle it under the egg and gently flip it over onto the plate. Turn off the stove.
7) Take the toast out of the toaster and butter it.
8) Serve with the egg.

Take about 15 minutes to prepare the **Pot Roast**. Get the following items:

Ingredients	Tools
1 medium carrot	crock pot
1 stalk celery	cutting board
½ medium brown onion	knife
¼ yellow bell pepper	spatula
1 kale leaf	measuring cup
2 tablespoon olive oil	
1 lb. roast beef	
1/4 teaspoon minced garlic	
1 tablespoon sweet paprika	
¼ teaspoon flaxseed	
½ teaspoon Salt	
¼ teaspoon Pepper	
Small lime wedge	
¼ cup water	
large bay leaf	

1) Begin by using the knife and cutting board to chop the carrot, celery, onion, bell pepper and kale, each in 4-5 pieces. Put them into the crock pot. Add the water and drizzle in the olive oil.
2) Cut the roast into 4 pieces and put in cooker on top of the vegetables. Sprinkle in the garlic, paprika, flaxseed, salt, pepper and squeeze in the lime. Toss the meat to mix in the spice.
3) Cover and turn it on high.
4) You are finished for now; you can leave it cooking for the next 8 hours.

Make sure you put away all items, leftovers are wrapped or stored and sealed in containers, clean up your up dishes, wipe down the table and cooking areas.

Lunch

Prep time: about 10 minutes

✔ Medications are best taken at least 45 minutes before meals. If the prescription specifies they are to be taken with food, then serve them with the meal instead.

<u>Day Two</u>

<u>**Place on the table**</u>
A small fork, table knife, glass of water, napkin and facial tissue.

Tuna Melt with Peaches

<u>Ingredients</u>	<u>Tools</u>
5 oz. can albacore tuna in water	cutting board
2 slices high fiber bread	knife to cut with
1 leaf of green leaf lettuce	measuring spoons
1 slice cheddar cheese	can opener
½ stalk celery	small fork
mayonnaise	small bowl
2 slices of bread	small spoon
peaches (already cut up)	butter knife
	small frying pan
	spatula
	dinner plate

1) Place the celery on the cutting board. Using the knife, cut it into very small pieces. Put it into the small bowl and set aside.

2) Open the can of tuna. Using the fork, scrape it into the bowl with the celery.
3) Add 2 tablespoons **mayonnaise** and using the fork, mix together until all of the tuna is coated with some mayonnaise. Chunks are okay.
4) Put two slices of bread onto the cutting board. Lightly spread mayonnaise on the bread and then flip it over and spread mayonnaise on one slice.
5) Put the frying pan on the stove and turn onto medium heat. Let it warm up and continue.
6) Spoon some of the tuna mixture onto the other slice of bread and spread it to the edges of the bread. You don't have to use all of it, just cover the bread to the edges. Then place a slice of cheddar on top of it.
7) Put the other slice of bread on the tuna to put the sandwich together.
8) Place the sandwich in the pan and let it heat for about 3 minutes.
9) Using your spatula, flip it over in the pan. It should be golden brown. If not, turn it over and leave it for another minute to get it golden, then flip it and brown the other side.
10) When the bread is golden brown, use the spatula to flip it onto the cutting board.
11) Cut the knife into 4 pieces and place on the plate next to the peaches.
12) Turn off the stove!

Remember, put everything away, clean up your dishes and wipe down the counters.

<u>Afternoon Snack</u>

Today might be a great day for some red grapes.

Prep time for today's dinner is about an hour, so if you plan on eating at 6 pm you need to start around 5, one hour prior.

<u>Dinner</u>

Prep time: Less than an hour

✓ Medications are best taken at least 45 minutes before meals. If the prescription specifies they are to be taken with food, then serve them with the meal instead.

> #### <u>Place on the table</u>
> A knife, fork, glass of water, napkin and facial tissue.

First thing, turn **off the crockpot. Do not remove the lid, just let it rest.** Then begin by preparing the sides. Wash your hands first.

Day Two

Ingredients	Tools
small russet potato	medium size slicing knife
6 or seven broccoli florets	cutting board
butter	potato peeler
milk	small fork
olive oil	large cooking spoon
½ lemon	small saucepan with lid
salt and pepper	oven mitts
	potato masher
	measuring spoons
	medium fryer/sauté pan

1) Using the potato peeler, peel the potato
2) Take the knife and cut the potato in six pieces and put them in the saucepan.
3) Fill the pan with water until the potatoes are covered. Add ¼ teaspoon of salt and on high heat on the stove.
4) Bring it to a boil.
5) Boil for about 20 minutes or until soft (you can check them with a fork).
6) Turn off the stove.

While the potatoes are cooking you can do the broccoli.

1) Put the sauté pan on the stove over medium heat and add 2 tablespoons olive oil
2) Add the broccoli and stir with spoon to coat it with the oil.
3) Continue to cook, while stirring occasionally for about 5 minutes.
4) Add about 2 tablespoons water and squeeze in the lemon. Keep cooking until tender, stirring occasionally.
5) Turn the burner off, add the salt and pepper, and put the lid on the pan. Let it sit while getting the dinner together. You do want the broccoli to be soft and this will keep it warm.

You are almost done....ready to prep the pot roast!! You will need to get:

Tools	
oven mitt	blender
measuring spoons	spatula
large fork	slicing knife
cutting board	large slotted spoon
medium size bowl	dinner plates

1) Using the oven mitt, open the lid from the cooker, remove the meat and place it on the cutting board, cover it with the lid to keep it warm.
2) Remove the bay leaf and discard it.
3) Using the slotted spoon, scoop the vegetables into blender.
4) Put the lid on and blend it on mix button until smooth. The mixture will be thick, so you can take some of the drippings from the meat and add it to the mixture, blending again each time until a desired gravy consistency is reached.
5) Slice off the desired amount of meat onto the (about 2 ounces of meat) placing the slices next to each other, in a row.
6) Scoop out about ½ pf the mashed potatoes and place on the plate next to the meat. Make a little indentation in the potatoes for some gravy. Pour the gravy from the blender over the meat and the potatoes.
7) Put 3 to 4 pieces of broccoli on the other side of the plate.

Now pour your beverages because you are ready to plate your food and eat!

Serve and enjoy! It will be worth the work.

Pot Roast with Mashed Potatoes and Broccoli

<u>Day Two</u>

There will be leftover meat and gravy. Put these in a sealed container in the refrigerator to use for another day's meal!

Ice cream will be a welcome dessert for tonight. You can add chocolate or fruit, or just sprinkles. But I suggest you avid whipped cream. Though many seniors need their calories, there is enough animal fat in this meal already!

Vanilla Ice Cream with Chocolate Chips and Raspberries

And, finally...clean up all of the dishes and clean the counter! Remember the dishwasher is your friend.

Day Three

First Thing!

✓ Medications are best taken at least 45 minutes before meals. If the prescription specifies they are to be taken with food, then serve them with the meal instead.

Menu

Breakfast	Lunch	Dinner
Oatmeal	Navy Bean Soup	Mom's Favorite Salad
Raisins	Crackers	Rosemary Chicken
Walnuts		Green Beans
Grape juice		Brown Rice

Afternoon snack: Red Grapes

Breakfast

Prep time: about 7 minutes

> **Place on the table**
> A spoon, a juice glass, a glass of water, napkin and facial tissue.

Ingredients	Tools
1 cup water	measuring cup
dash salt	measuring spoons
½ cup rolled oats	quart size Pot
¼ teaspoon flaxseed	large spoon
1/4 cup rice milk	cereal bowl
1 tablespoon raisins	
maple syrup or brown sugar	
cranberry juice	
walnuts optional	

1) Put the pan on the burner, add water and salt and turn burner onto high heat. Bring it to a boil.
2) Once boiling, stir in the oatmeal then turn the burner down to medium heat. Cook about 5 minutes, or until all of the water is absorbed and oatmeal is soft. Turn off the stove.
3) Use the large spoon to scoop the oatmeal into a bowl. Pour the milk over it. Sprinkle on the flaxseed and drizzle with syrup or brown sugar, as desired. Lastly, sprinkle the raisins over the oatmeal.
4) Pour the juice and serve any coffee or tea.

Oatmeal with Raisins and Walnuts

Lunch

Prep time: about 25 minutes

✓ Medications are best taken at least 45 minutes before meals. If the prescription specifies they are to be taken with food, then serve them with the meal instead.

Place on the table
A soup spoon, glass of water, napkin and facial tissue.

Ingredients	Tools
2 pieces ham	chopping knife
2/3 cup chopped onion	cutting board
I stalk celery	measuring cup
1 small carrot	measuring spoons
½ teaspoon minced garlic	large saucepan with a lid
2 tablespoons olive oil	large spoon
1 small leaf kale, remove stem	oven mitt
1 – 16 ounce cans navy beans, drained	blender
¼ teaspoon thyme	soup ladle
1/8 teaspoon ground pepper	soup bowl
1 teaspoon chopped parsley	
16 ounces of chicken broth	
high fiber crackers	

Navy Bean Soup

1) On the cutting board, cut the ham into small pieces, about ¼ to ½ inches in size. Put in the measuring cup. It should be about ½ cup of meat. If not at least ½ cup, you can cut more ham if you like.
2) Next, coarsely chop onion, celery, and carrot, and mince the garlic. Then finely chop the kale and measure to 2 tablespoons.
3) Put the large saucepan on the stove, add the olive oil, and turn the burner to medium high heat. Add the meat, all the vegetables and garlic. Stir and cook for about 5 minutes.
4) Turn the heat down to medium and add the beans, chicken broth and thyme. Stir again.
5) Bring it to a boil, and then turn down the heat to medium-low, keeping it to a low boil and stir once more. Place the lid partially over the top of the pan, allowing for some steam to escape. Cook for 20 minutes. This allows the meat flavor to infuse in the soup.
6) After 20 minutes, turn the heat off, put an oven mitt on, remove the pan from the heat and place it on a cold burner on the stove. Let it sit for about 5 minutes. Then, again with the oven mitt, remove the lid from the pan.
7) Take the lid off the blender, and using the soup ladle, put half of the soup in the blender. Place the lid on the blender and hit the lowest speed (mix) for about 15 seconds. Blending part of the soup with the veggies gives it a creamy texture.
8) Return this to the pan and mix together with the rest of the soup. Stir in the pepper and salt to taste. Turn off the stove.
9) Using the soup ladle, scoop the soup into the bowl.
10) Serve with favorite soup crackers or bread and a glass of water.

Day Three

Remember: clean up all of the dishes and put your ingredients and tools away, and wipe the countertops and area clean keeping it germ free. Make sure all leftovers are stored in sealed container and put in the refrigerator.

Afternoon Snack

Put out a bowl of mixed dried fruit to snack on. If it's a hot summer day, ice cream is a welcome treat!

Dinner
Prep time about 45 minutes

✓ Medications are best taken at least 45 minutes before meals. If the prescription specifies they are to be taken with food, then serve them with the meal instead.

Place on the table
A knife, fork, glass of water, napkin and facial tissue.

Start dinner by first preparing the Rosemary Chicken. Note that you are making enough chicken to use again for day 6 lunch. You will need the following items:

Ingredients	Tools
6 chicken thighs	glass baking pan
olive oil	2 paper towels
2 tablespoon rosemary	measuring spoons
1 teaspoon oregano	medium mixing bowl
1/2 teaspoon onion powder	salad tongs
½ of a lemon	oven mitts
salt and pepper	salad bowl
¼ cup grated parmesan cheese	dinner plate

1) Preheat the oven to 375 degrees.
2) Rinse the chicken with water and place it on the paper towels to absorb excess water. Place it in the medium mixing bowl.
3) Add 2 tablespoons olive oil, the rosemary, oregano, onion powder and lemon zest into the bowl over the chicken.
4) Using the salad tongs, toss the chicken until well coated. (You can use your hands if you want, but just make sure you wash them well before you do!)

5) Place the chicken in the baking pan, and sprinkle the thighs with salt and pepper.
6) Slice the lemon into circle, then cut in pieces and scatter them over the chicken in the pan. Sprinkle with the parmesan cheese.
7) Place the pan in the oven (uncovered).
8) Put timer on for 45 minutes.

Rosemary Chicken ready for the oven

Make sure you wash everything well with hot water, especially your hands because you're handling raw poultry.

While the chicken is baking, get the following items:

Ingredients	Tools
¼ medium sweet onion	cutting board
olive oil	comfortable knife to chop with
½ teaspoon salt	measuring spoon
1¼ cup water	measuring cup
½ cup brown rice	quart size pot with the lid
	large spoon

Once you have everything in front of you:

1) Use the knife on the cutting board to chop the onion into small pieces

2) Place the saucepan on the stove, add the olive oil, turn the heat on medium/high and add the onions. Cook and stir until the onions look slightly clear. .

3) Add the water and salt and bring it to a boil.

4) Once boiling, add the rice, stir with the spoon and bring to a boil again.

5) Cover with the lid and turn the heat down to the lowest heat to simmer.

Next, make the green beans. You already have some items, your cutting board, measuring spoons, olive oil, and salt. But will need to get the following items:

Ingredients	Tools
16 -18 fresh green beans	paring knife
2 tablespoons water	sautee pan
Pepper	cooking tongs

1) On the cutting board, use the paring knife to cut the stem off the beans. Slice the beans into 2 inch long pieces (bites size!)

2) Place the sauté pan on the stove and put the olive oil in it.

3) Turn the heat on medium and toss in the green beans. Stir the beans around for about a minute, getting them well coated with the oil.

4) Add the water, and then let them cook for about 8 more minutes.

5) Meanwhile, move on to the next step and make the salad.

Next, get the salad dressing out of the refrigerator. Hopefully you have already made the **basic olive oil & vinegar salad dressing** and it's in the refrigerator. If not, the recipe is on page 58.

Then get the following items:

Ingredients	Tools
4 leaves of romaine	knife to chop with
1 cup of iceberg lettuce	cutting board
red grape or cherry tomatoes	medium bowl
½ cucumber, peeled	2 spatulas, large spoons or
2 slices red onion	tongs for tossing
salt and pepper	

When you have everything ready:

1) Using the large knife on cutting board, chop the romaine and iceberg into bite size pieces and place it in the bowl. You may use your hands and tear the lettuce if it is easier. But note that making the pieces small and bite size..
2) On the cutting board take the cucumber, and, slice it into bite size pieces. It does not matter how you do this. I suggest you slice the cucumber in small disks, then cut those in half 2 times making about 1 inch sized pieces.
3) Take the red onion and slice off one ¼ inch thick piece. Cut it in half and chop into small pieces.
4) If the cherry tomatoes are large, slice them in half as well.
5) Place the cucumbers, onion and tomatoes in the medium bowl over the lettuce.
6) Pour some dressing as desired and toss using the tongs.
7) Put half of the salad mixture in each salad bowl.
8) Turn the heat off under the beans in the other pan on the stove, but let them sit.
9) You can place the salad on the table and begin eating! You should be able to finish the salad before the chicken is done.

Rosemary Chicken on Brown Rice with Green Beans

When the oven timer goes off....

<u>Day Three</u>

1) Turn the oven off. Get a piece of aluminum foil about 10 inches long. Put your oven mitts on and take the chicken out of the oven. Thighs should be a nice golden brown.
2) Put the pan on the stove top on a burner you are **not** using. Put about 2 tablespoons of water in the chicken droppings and place the foil over the chicken to hold the steam in for a few minutes until serving.
3) Next, turn off the heat under the rice. With oven mitts on, remove the lid from that pot.
4) Using your large spoon, stir the rice. It should be soft, fluffy and ready to serve. Put the lid back on until you are ready to put the food on the plate. (If the rice is still too firm, add ¼ cup of hot water and continue to simmer about 5 more minutes, with the lid on the pan until the rice is soft and ready to serve).
5) If you haven't finished your salad, do that now and clear the salad bowls.
6) Then, with your oven mitt on, scoop out some rice onto the dinner plate.
7) Using your tongs, place a piece of chicken on top of the rice.
8) Use your tongs to some beans on the plate.
9) For the final step, take a spatula and scrape the pan mixing the water with the chicken drippings. Using a spoon, drizzle each piece of chicken with some of the drippings, then serve.
10) Make sure the stove is turned off!

After dinner, be sure to put away the chicken and store it in a sealed container because you will be using the leftovers in a couple of days. Serve a dessert. A cupcake is always a welcome treat!

Remember! Clean up the table, countertop and wash the dishes. If you have a dishwasher, put all of the dishes in and turn it on!

Day Four

First Thing!

✓ Medications are best taken at least 45 minutes before meals. If the prescription specifies they are to be taken with food, then serve them with the meal instead.

Menu

Breakfast	Lunch	Dinner
Raisin Bran	Chopped Greens	Pico de Gallo
Flaxseed	Salmon Salad	Beef Tacos
Rice Milk	Sandwich	Guacamole
Apricot Nectar		Chips and Salsa
		Ice Cream

Afternoon snack: Red Grapes

Breakfast

Prep time: 3 minutes

Place on the table
A spoon, juice glass, glass of water, napkin, facial tissue.

Get these things together:

Ingredients	Tools
raisin bran	cereal bowl
¼ teaspoon flaxseed	small glass
rice milk	measuring spoons
honey	

1) Pour the desired amount of raisin bran into the cereal bowl and pour the rice milk over it.
2) Sprinkle the flaxseed over the cereal and drizzle with honey for desired sweetness.
3) Open the can of apricot nectar and pour it into the glass.
4) You are ready to serve.

Make sure you put away all items and clean up the breakfast dishes before moving on with your day!

Day Four

Lunch

Prep time: about 15 minutes

✓ Medications are best taken at least 45 minutes before meals. If the prescription specifies they are to be taken with food, then serve them with the meal instead.

> **Place on the table**
> A small fork, spoon glass of water, napkin and facial tissue.

Start lunch by getting the following things together:

Ingredients	Tools
4 pieces dark kale	cutting board
4 pieces collard greens	chopping knife
4 pieces green leaf lettuce	large bowl
2/3 cucumber – peeled	blender
1 stalk celery	rubber spatula
1/2 bell pepper (preferably mild in flavor, yellow or orange)	lemon juicer
2 tablespoons basil	measuring spoons
2 tablespoons cilantro	food storage container with lid
olive oil and vinegar salad dressing	2 small bowls
¼ of a lemon	

Once you have the above items,

1) Tear the kale, collard green and leaf lettuce in approximately 2 inch pieces. Put them in the blender.
2) Use your knife on the cutting board to cut the cucumber, bell peppers and celery into approximately 1 inch chunks. Put them into the blender and place the lid on the blender.
3) Holding the lid on with one hand, hit the pulse button on the blender 2 to 3 times to chop ingredients.
4) Take the lid off the blender and using your spatula, scrape the ingredients off the inside of the carafe. Put the lid on the blender.
5) Pulse again once or twice. Everything should be well chopped.
6) Take the lid off the blender, and using your spatula, scrape the ingredients into the large bowl.
7) Add olive oil, vinegar and lemon juice and mix it up with your spatula.
8) Add salt and pepper to taste.

9) This may yield more greens than you eat at one meal. Put the leftover greens in a covered Tupperware container as you will use them again in a couple of days.

Note: 1/2 can of garbanzo beans can be mixed in and served with whole grain toast to make a complete meal. Or, you can skip the chicken sandwich and put the chicken on the salad with the beans.

| *Chopped Greens* | *Salmon Salad Sandwich* |

If desired, get the following items together to make the sandwich:

Ingredients	Tools
leftover salmon from day one	cereal bowl
¼ stalk celery, chopped	small spoon
1 dill pickle slice	small fork
1 tablespoon mayonnaise	cutting board
salt and pepper	knife to chop and cut with
2 slices bread	

* Don't panic if someone ate the salmon and there is no leftover fish. Canned salmon makes a nice sandwich

1) Place the salmon into the bowl and chop it up with the fork.
2) Finely chop the celery and add it and the mayonnaise to the salmon. Mix it together with your fork.
3) Add a dash of salt, pepper and onion powder. Mix it together. You can add more mayonnaise to taste.
4) Clean off the cutting board and put the two slices of bread on it.

5) Scoop out the salmon mixture and spread it on one of the slices of bread. You don't have to use all of it, just cover the bread to the edges.
6) Place the lettuce on top, cover with the other slice of bread and cut the sandwich in half.
7) Place it on the plate and serve with your salad. You are ready to eat!

Clean up your mess, put away your tools and put your leftovers in the refrigerator!

Afternoon Snack

A couple of hours after lunch set out some oatmeal cookies. If you haven't made them yet, and have time to make them, the recipe is on page 59.

Oatmeal Cookies

Dinner

Prep time: 20 minutes

✓ Medications are best taken at least 45 minutes before meals. If the prescription specifies they are to be taken with food, then serve them with the meal instead.

> **Place on the table**
> A fork, glass of water, napkin and facial tissue.

Day Four

Beef Taco with Pico de Gallo, Guacamole, Salsa and Chips

Ingredients	Tools
2 avocados	knife to slice
lime	knife to chop with
jalapeño	cutting board
medium sized onion	small spoon
½ teaspoon ground cumin	dinner fork
cilantro	small mixing bowl
1 teaspoon mayonnaise	small bowl
ground cayenne pepper	
A tomato	

Gather everything you need for the guacamole:

1) Take your knife and insert it into the avocados in a circle all the way around the center of each one. You should be able to feel the pit inside.
2) Open the avocados by holding them like a ball, twisting and pulling them apart
3) Insert the knife into the pit, pull it out and throw it away.
4) Take your spoon and scoop out all of the avocado meat into the bowl.
5) Using your fork, mash the avocado until it is smooth with some small chunks.
6) Using your knife, on the cutting board, take the jalapeño and trim off the stem. Then slice it in half, dig out and discard the seeds.
7) Finely chop the jalapeño.

8) Chop the onion.
9) Next, chop about a 3/4 cup of cilantro.
10) Take half of each of the jalapeño and onion as well as 1/3 of the cilantro and put it into the bowl with the avocado.
11) Cut the lime into 4 wedges. Squeeze two of the lime wedges into the bowl.
12) Add the cumin and stir.
13) Using the fork, mix everything together.
14) Taste the mixture. Add salt if desired.

*Adding cayenne pepper is optional, as it will make it hot and spicy. Then take a teaspoon of mayonnaise and spread it on top of the mixture, place a piece of cellophane over the top and put it in the refrigerator until dinner is served. The mayonnaise will keep the guacamole from turning brown as it spoils quickly.

Now you are ready to make the Pico de Gallo.

Ingredients	**Tools**
leftover roast beef (from pot roast)	medium frying pan with a lid
¼ yellow pepper*	large cooking spoon
olive oil	oven mitts
½ teaspoon ground cumin	dinner plate
corn tortillas	
lettuce	
cheddar cheese	
corn chips	

*You should have leftover pepper from other days. If you do not, then you can use red pepper or skip the pepper altogether

1) Using the slicing knife, cut out the brown core stem on the top of the tomato.
2) Put the tomato on the cutting board and cut it in half.
3) Take each half and cut it into ¼ inch to ½ inch chunks.
4) Scrape them into the bowl and add half each of the jalapeño and onion, and cilantro.
5) Squeeze in one lime wedge and toss with a spoon.
6) Put it aside.

Next, make the tacos:

Day Four

1) Chop the yellow pepper into small pieces.
2) Put the pan on the stove over a medium to high heat. Add 2 tablespoons of olive oil and let it heat up for about 30 seconds
3) Add the onion, jalapeño and yellow pepper.
4) With the large spoon, mix it together, then turn the heat to low, cooking until the onions look clear.
5) Meanwhile, cut the roast beef it into small chunks.
6) Once the onions look clear, add the roast beef to the pan and combine it into the mixture. Add the cumin, and stir again.
7) Squeeze the lime over the mixture, and stir again.
8) Add any cayenne pepper as desired.
9) Turn the heat off and set aside.
10) Place the lid on the pan.

Now you are ready to make the tacos and put it all together on a plate.

1) Get the guacamole and salsa out of the refrigerator.
2) Put 4 corn tortillas on the cutting board.
3) With the small spoon, smear some guacamole into the middle of each tortilla.
4) Spoon out some meat mixture.
5) Sprinkle it with some of the remaining cilantro and some cheddar cheese.
6) Fold in half and place 2 on each plate with some corn chips, guacamole and Pico de Gallo as garnish.
7) Don't forget to serve juice, water, or even some milk or soda with this zesty meal!

Your favorite ice cream makes a good dessert after a meal that has some heat or spice.

Enjoy your evening! Remember, you will enjoy it even more if you clean up the dishes and food immediately after dinner...then you can really relax!

Day Five

First Thing!

✓ Medications are best taken at least 45 minutes before meals. If the prescription specifies they are to be taken with food, then serve them with the meal instead.

Menu

Breakfast	Lunch	Dinner*
Oatmeal Rice Milk Flaxseed Berries	Romaine and Avocado Salad Salmon Salad Sandwich	Mom's Favorite Salad Boneless Pork Chops with Mushrooms Cauliflower Any Dessert
Afternoon Snack: Dried Fruit		

*Morning prep time is needed as pork chops are cooked in the crock pot

Breakfast

Prep time: 5 minutes

Place on the table
A spoon, glass of water, napkin, facial tissue.

Ingredients	Tools
1 cup water ½ cup rolled oats ¼ teaspoon flaxseed 1/4 cup rice milk 1 tablespoon raisins maple syrup or brown sugar cranberry juice walnuts optional	measuring cup measuring spoons quart size saucepan large spoon cereal bowl

5) Put the pan on the burner and add water. Turn burner onto high heat and bring it to a boil.
6) Once boiling, stir in the oatmeal then turn the burner down to medium heat. Cook about 5 minutes, or until all of the water is absorbed and oatmeal is soft.

7) Use the large spoon to scoop the oatmeal into a bowl. Pour the milk over it, sprinkle on the flaxseed and drizzle with syrup or brown sugar, as desired. Lastly, sprinkle the raisins over the oatmeal.

8) Pour the juice and serve any coffee or tea requested.

Clean up all of your items from breakfast. Keep the tongs, cutting board, paring knife, and oven mitts you will need these for dinner.

Lunch

Prep time: about 10 minutes

✓ Medications are best taken at least 45 minutes before meals. If the prescription specifies they are to be taken with food, then serve them with the meal instead.

Ham and Cheese Sandwich with Romaine Salad

> ### Place on the table
> A knife, fork, glass of water, napkin and facial tissue.

Start lunch by making the salad:

Ingredients	Tools
6 leaves of romaine	knife to chop with
¼ cucumber, peeled	cutting board
½ avocado	medium bowl
italian dressing	salad tongs for tossing
salt and pepper	salad bowl

10) Using your hands, tear the romaine into bite size pieces and put place them in the bowl.
11) On the cutting board, slice the cucumber into bite size pieces. Put the cucumber in the bowl with the romaine.
12) Insert the knife into the avocado until it hits the pit. Holding it onto the pit, slide the knife around the outside of the avocado and pull it in half. Remove the pit.
13) Cut each in half again to make 4 pieces total. Then remove the peel.
14) On the cutting board, cut the avocado into small chunks and place them in the bowl over the romaine.
15) Put the dressing over the lettuce and toss with the salad tongs.
16) Using the tongs put the salad in the bowls and place on the table while making the sandwich.

Ingredients	Tools
2 slices of ham	cutting board
one slice cheddar cheese	knife to cut with
mustard	butter knife
mayonnaise	small frying pan
2 slices of bread	cooking spatula

1) Put two slices of bread onto the cutting board. Lightly spread mayonnaise on both pieces of bread. Turn it over and spread mustard on one slice.
2) Put the frying pan on the stove and turn onto medium heat. Let it warm up and continue.
3) Place a slice of cheddar, then 2 slices of ham on one piece of bread and put the other slice of bread over the other, mayonnaise side out, to put the sandwich together.
4) Place the sandwich in the pan and let it heat for about 3 minutes.
5) Using your spatula, flip it over in the pan. It should be golden brown. If not, turn it over and leave it for another minute to get it golden, then flip it and brown the other side.
6) Using the spatula, flip the sandwich back to the cutting board and cut it into 4 pieces. Serve!

Day Five

You will enjoy your afternoon more if you don't have dishes to do before dinner, so clean up everything from lunch and put it away!

Afternoon Snack

Even if you have to go out for the afternoon, dried fruit is a great snack as you can put it out and not worry about it spoiling. Whatever I left in the cupboard is fine.

Dinner
Prep time: 20 minutes

Pork Roast with Cauliflower and Salad

✓ Medications are best taken at least 45 minutes before meals. If the prescription specifies they are to be taken with food, then serve them with the meal instead.

> **Place on the table**
> A knife, fork, glass of water, napkin and facial tissue.

Day Five

You will need the following items for dinner prep:

Ingredients	Tools
3 boneless pork chops	large sauté pan and lid
olive oil	chopping knife
½ lb. portobello mushroom	cutting board
½ celery stalk	small paring knife
½ an onion	measuring spoons
1 teaspoon thyme	measuring cup
1/2 cup stock (vegetable or chicken)	tongs
	paper towels
1 tablespoon flour*	oven mitts
salt and pepper	large spoon

The kind of flour you use is your choice. You can use gluten free mix, arrowroot, or regular wheat flour.

1) Put your ½ onion on the cutting board. Make sure all of the outer skin is removed.
2) Slice the onion chop the slices into small pieces, put aside.
3) Slice the celery stalks lengthwise and chop them into small pieces.
4) Clean the mushroom and cut it into bite sized pieces.
5) Take the pork chops, rinse them with cold water and pat dry with the paper towels. Place them on the cutting board. With the small knife, trim the fat off around the edges. Wash your hands.
6) Put the pan on the stove, add 2 tablespoons olive oil. Turn the heat onto medium high and let the oil heat up for about 30 seconds. You will know it is getting hot when you see the oil start to move in the pan.
7) We are going to sear the meat by placing it in the hot oil. It should sizzle when it hits the pan. If it doesn't, then use your tongs to remove the meat and wait a little longer.
8) Let the meat fry in the oil for about 2 minutes. Using your tongs, turn the meat over in the pan. You can now add the onion, celery and mushroom.
9) Let them all cook on medium high, stirring the vegetable, for about 2 minutes.
10) Turn the heat down to low or a simmer and add the thyme.
11) Turn the meat over and stir the vegetables one last time. Add the stock, stir once more and cover the pan.
12) Let it simmer for about 30 minutes with the lid on.

Day Five

In the meantime, make the cauliflower.

Ingredients	Tools
7-8 cauliflower florets	sauté or large frying pan with a lid
2 tablespoons olive oil	large spoon
1/4 lemon	dinner plate
salt and pepper	

1) Put the pan over a medium high heat and add the oil.
2) Once the oil is hot, add the cauliflower and toss it well in the oil. Cook for about 5 minutes, tossing it about every 30 seconds.
3) Add the salt, pepper and 1 tablespoon water. Squeeze in the lemon.
4) Turn the heat down to simmer and put the lid on the pan.
5) It will keep cooking and get softer the while you get the salad ready.

Ingredients	Tools
6 leaves of romaine	comfortable knife to cut with
¼ cucumber	potato peeler
½ avocado	cutting board
italian dressing	small salad bowl
salt and pepper	salad tongs for tossing
1 teaspoon sesame seed	

1) Use your knife and the cutting board to chop the romaine into bite size pieces. Place them in the bowl. (You may tear them by hand if it is easier.)
2) Take the cucumber, peel it with the peeler. Slice it into bite size pieces and place them on top of the romaine.
3) Remove the pit from the avocado. With the skin on, hold half of the avocado with one hand while slicing through it making a checkerboard pattern with the knife. Then pushing form the peel side of the avocado, push it inside out and the pieces will fall into the bowl. You can scrape them off with a spoon if the avocado is too soft doesn't fall out on its own.
4) Add the Italian dressing and toss with the tongs. Sprinkle the top with sesame seeds.
5) You can sit down and eat your salad while the meat is still cooking. The longer you let it cook, it becomes more and more tender.

Getting the pork ready:

1) With the oven mitts, remove the pan from the heat and let it sit for about 2 minutes.
2) Meanwhile, put the flour into the measuring cup and add about ¼ cup water. Mix the flour and water together.
3) Remove the lid from the pan stir the ingredients with your spoon.
4) Using your tongs, take the meat out of the pan and place it on the cutting board.
5) Put the pan back on the heat and add the flour mixture, stirring it into the gravy until it thickens. Then remove the pan from the heat and turn off the stove.
6) Turn the heat off under the cauliflower
7) Take you knife and slice the chops into long small pieces, or however you need to cut it for your loved one. Place the meat nicely on the plate. Put some cauliflower on the plate next to the meet.
8) With your spoon, scoop up some of the mushrooms, onions and sauce and pour it over the meat and cauliflower.
9) You are ready to eat!

Chocolate Ice Cream with chocolate chips
and whipped cream

Enjoy your evening! Remember, you will enjoy it even more if you clean up the dishes and food immediately after dinner…then you can really relax.

Day Seven

First Thing!

✓ Medications are best taken at least 45 minutes before meals. If the prescription specifies they are to be taken with food, then serve them with the meal instead.

Menu

Breakfast	Lunch	Dinner
Raisin Bran	Chopped Greens	Pan Seared Fish
Rice Milk	Chicken Salad	Tartar Sauce
Berries	Sandwich	Roasted Broccoli
Apricot Nectar	Grapes	And Potatoes
		Cupcake
Afternoon Snack: Red Grapes		

Breakfast

Prep time: 3 minutes

> ### Place on the table
> A spoon, glass of water, napkin, facial tissue.

Begin by getting the following items:

Ingredients	Tools
½ cup raisin bran cereal	cereal bowl
¼ teaspoon flaxseed	small glass
rice milk	measuring spoons
honey	

5) Pour the raisin bran into the cereal bowl and pour the rice milk over it.
6) Sprinkle the flaxseed over the cereal and drizzle with honey for desired sweetness.
7) Open the can of apricot nectar and pour it into the glass.
8) You are ready to serve breakfast.

Make sure you put away all items and clean up the breakfast dishes before moving on with your day!

Day Seven

Lunch

Prep time: about 15 minutes

✓ Medications are best taken at least 45 minutes before meals. If the prescription specifies they are to be taken with food, then serve them with the meal instead.

> ### Place on the table
> A knife, fork, glass of water, napkin and facial tissue.

Chicken Salad Sandwich with Greens and Grapes

Ingredients	Tools
leftover rosemary chicken thighs	small bowl
½ stalk celery	cutting board
½ small avocado	small spoon
2 tablespoons olive oil mayonnaise	small fork
2 slices whole grain, or fiber bread	chopping knife
lettuce- any type	medium bowl
	plate

1) Start by separating the chicken from the skin and discarding the skin.
2) Place the chicken on the cutting board and cut it into very small pieces. Put it into the small bowl and set aside.
3) Finely chop the celery and add to the chicken.

4) Clean off the cutting board and put the two slices of bread on it
5) Place the mayonnaise and avocado into the medium bowl. Mash them together with a fork until it is somewhat creamy. Some chunks are okay. Add the chicken and salt, and mix it together.
6) Using your spatula, put the chicken mixture on one of the slices of bread and spread it. You don't have to use all of it, just cover the bread to the edges.
7) Place the lettuce on top. Spread some mayonnaise on the other slice of bread and put it onto the lettuce.
8) Cut it in half and put it on the plate with the greens.
9) You are ready to eat! Cleanup your dishes!

Afternoon Snack

Oatmeal cookies are an easy snack. And they are yummy as well as healthy!

Dinner

Prep time: about 30 minutes

✓ Medications are best taken at least 45 minutes before meals. If the prescription specifies they are to be taken with food, then serve them with the meal instead.

Pan Seared Cod with Roasted Broccoli and Redskins
Left-over Green Beans and Rice

Day Seven

Today, look through the refrigerator and pull out any leftover rice, or vegetables. Heat them in a saucepan with a lid on the stove. You can do that now, turn the heat to low, and putting on the lid. If it is the brown rice you are warming up, add some water and stir before heating.

Ingredients	Tools
8- 10 broccoli florets 4 small redskin potatoes olive oil salt	cutting board chopping knife metal baking pan cooking spatula oven mitts

Place on the table
A knife, fork, glass of water, napkin and facial tissue.

Next, make the sides. Get the following items:
1) Preheat the oven to 375 degrees.
2) Broccoli should already be cut and cleaned, so put them in the baking pan.
3) Next, rinse the potatoes and cut them in bite sized pieces.
4) Place these in the pan with the broccoli, olive oil and salt. Toss it together.
5) Place the pan into the oven and set the timer for 30 minutes.

Ingredients	Tools
2 tablespoons olive oil 1 teaspoon paprika ¼ teaspoon onion powder 2 teaspoons dill weed 1/2 of a lemon light drizzle of honey 3/4 pound filet of fish	measuring spoons large frying pan with a lid spatula oven mitt

1) Rinse the fish with cold water and place between paper towels and pat dry
2) Place the pan on the stove; add the olive oil, paprika and onion powder.
3) Take the lemon and using the grater, grate the lemon rind into the pan.
4) Wait until the timer goes off for the oven vegetables. Then turn off the oven, but don't take the pan out yet.
5) Turn on the heat under the pan on the stove to medium high. Let it heat until you see the ingredients begin to slightly sizzle.
6) Lightly drizzle some honey into the pan, and sprinkle in the dill weed.

7) Then add the fish (skin up if there is skin on it), letting it sear for about a minute.

8) Turn the heat down to medium low and put the lid on the pan.

9) Depending on the fish you choose, let it cook for up to 5 minutes. If you use sole, or thin tilapia, you only need to cook about one more minute and you are done. Otherwise, continue to the next step.

10) Wearing an oven mitt, remove the lid, and turn over the fish in lime pan.

11) Put the lid back on and continue to cook for another minute then remove the pan from the heat and put your oven mitts on and take the pan out of the oven.

12) The vegetables should be crispy on the outside and tender in the middle.

13) With the spatula, scoop a piece of fish onto the plate. Put about a tablespoon of tartare sauce on the side next to it, then spoon even amounts of broccoli and potatoes onto the plate.

14) You are ready to serve.

15) Clean up your dishes and ktichen!

Banana Cupcakes with Buttercream Frosting
One each topped with Blackberry, Raspberry and Lime Zest.

Day Seven

First Thing!

✓ Medications are best taken at least 45 minutes before meals. If the prescription specifies they are to be taken with food, then serve them with the meal instead.

Menu

Breakfast	Lunch	Dinner*
Fruit Smoothie	Frittata	Mom's Favorite Salad
Oatmeal	Fresh Melon	Cheeseburger
Rice Milk		Veggie Leftovers
Raisins		Dessert
Juice		

Afternoon Snack: Grapes

Breakfast

Prep time: 8 minutes

> **Place on the table**
> A spoon, glass of water, napkin, facial tissue.

Begin by getting the following items:

Ingredients	Tools
½ kale leaf	measuring cup
1/4 cup blueberries	cutting board
1/4 cup raspberries	blender
2 pieces frozen banana	water glass
1 teaspoon flaxseed	
½ cup rice milk	
honey	

10) Take the lid off of the blender. Tear the kale leaves in half and put all of the pieces in the blender.
11) Put in all of the fruit, the flaxseed, and rice milk. Add just a small dab of honey for sweetness.
12) Place the lid back on the blender and turn on to lowest speed until the ingredients are mixed together.

46

13) Then turn it up to the next highest speed, blend for 10 seconds, then to the next highest for 10 seconds and continue to the highest speed and blending until smooth and foamy.

14) Turn it off. Take the lid off and pour it into a glass. You are ready to serve.

While they are enjoying their smoothie, you can prepare the oatmeal. You need to get the following items.

Ingredients	Tools
1 cup water	measuring cup
½ cup rolled oats	measuring spoons
¼ teaspoon flaxseed	quart size pot
1/4 cup rice milk	large spoon
1 tablespoon raisins	cereal bowl
maple syrup	
grape juice	

1) Put the water and salt in the pan on high heat and bring it to a boil.

2) Once boiling, turn down the stove to medium heat and stir in the oatmeal, cooking approximately 5 minutes, or until all of the water is absorbed and oatmeal is soft.

3) Turn off the stove.

4) With your large spoon, scoop the oatmeal into the cereal bowl and pour the milk over it. Sprinkle on the flaxseed and drizzle with honey if desired. Put the raisins on top of the cereal.

5) Serve with juice *and* a glass of water.

After breakfast, be sure to put away all of your prep items clean up!

Lunch

Prep time approximately 15 minutes

✓ Medications are best taken at least 45 minutes before meals. If the prescription specifies they are to be taken with food, then serve them with the meal instead.

> ### Place on the table
> A knife, fork, glass of water, napkin and facial tissue.

Day Seven

Frittata with Toast and Peaches

Ingredients	Tools
2 tablespoons olives oil	small bowl
4 eggs	measuring spoons
½ an avocado	small fork or whisk
onion	paring knife
small bunch cilantro	large spatula
grated cheese	cutting board
1/2 teaspoon flaxseed	small spoon
1 tablespoon milk	medium frying pan with a lid
salt and pepper	
2 pieces of bread	
olive oil & butter spread	
any fruit or fruit cup	

1) Start by getting the 2 plates, and putting the fruit on each plate. Then place the plates out on the counter and Start making the frittata

2) On the cutting board, using the paring knife, take the onion and slice of a piece off, and cut into smaller pieces.

3) Put the pan on the stove, add one tablespoon of olive oil and turn the heat on medium. Add the onion and let it cook while you prepare the rest.

4) Take your avocado and scoop out the meat with your spoon onto the cutting board. Cut the avocado into small pieces. Let it sit.
5) Take your spatula and stir the onions cooking in the pan. Turn the heat up to medium high until the onions turn a bit milky white.
6) Crack the eggs into the small bowl, add one tablespoon of the olive oil and the milk. Beat with the whisk or the fork, until it looks light and fluffy. Then pour it into the pan. If it sizzles, you did it right! Turn the heat to medium low.
7) Tear the cilantro into as small of pieces (you can chop it if you like) and add it , the avocado, cheese, salt and pepper.
8) Place the lid one the pan and let it cook until the eggs sets up a bit solid on top.
9) Toast the bread.
10) Once the eggs set up, remove the lid, take your spatula and flip over the frittata.
11) Turn off the heat,
12) Slice it in half, butter it and place 2 halves on each plate.
13) Using a small knife, slice the frittata in half
14) Arrange it on the plate with the toast and fruit. Serve!

You made it this far. Clean up! It's a good thing to make this a habit.

Afternoon Snack

Oatmeal cookies again! Yum!

Dinner
Prep time 15 minutes

✓ Medications are best taken at least 45 minutes before meals. If the prescription specifies they are to be taken with food, then serve them with the meal instead.

You don't want to waste any food. So look in the refrigerator and see if there are any veggies or potatoes left. You can put these in a small pan and heat just before you serve, or substitute them for the salad.

> ### **Place on the table**
> A knife, fork, glass of water, napkin and facial tissue.

Day Seven

Start by making your salad. Get these items (you should know this one by now!):

Ingredients	Tools
4 leaves of romaine	comfortable knife to chop with
¼ head of iceberg lettuce	cutting board
red grape or cherry tomatoes	medium bowl
½ cucumber, peeled	2 spatulas, large spoons or
2 slices red onion	salad tongs for tossing
salt and pepper	

1) Chop the romaine and iceberg into bite size pieces. Put them in the bowl.
2) Slice the cucumber into bite size pieces. Put in the bowl.
3) Slice off one ¼ inch thick piece of onion and chop into bite size pieces. Put in the bowl
4) Cut the cherry tomatoes in half, and add them to the bowl.
5) Pour on italian dressing as desired and toss.
6) Put half of the salad mixture on each small salad plate.

Burger and Salad, with Watermelon garnish

Day Seven

Ingredients	Tools
leftover vegetables	small saucepan
½ pound ground beef	Spoon
¼ teaspoon flaxseed	medium bowl
slice of cheese	frying pan with a lid
Onion	spatula
whole grain bun	cutting board
dill chips (pickles)	small knife
mustard	an oven mitt
ketchup	
salt and pepper	

You can always serve this with corn chips or potato chips as a Saturday night treat.

1) Wash your hands.
2) Add the flaxseed to the burger and mix with your hands.
3) Separate the burger into 2 equal sized balls.
4) Put them on the cutting board and with your hands, press them down to a flat disc. You can use the spatula to make a final press. The flatter and thinner the better.
5) Next, Put the pan on the stove over a medium heat and put the meat in the pan.
6) Wash your hands again.
7) Take the onion and slice off a 2 pieces.
8) Place the onions in the pan with the meat.
9) Sprinkle the meat and onions very lightly with salt and pepper.
10) Let it fry until the meat turns brown on the sides. This will take about 3 minutes. Then using your spatula, flip over both the burger and the onions.
11) Let it cook for about a minute, then place the cheese on top. Put the lid on the pan so the cheese can melt.
12) Put the bun, open face, on the plate.
13) After about a minute, the cheese should be melted, use an oven mitt to take the lid of the pan.
14) Using your spatula, flip the burger and some onions onto the bun.
15) Add pickle, mustard and ketchup to taste.
16) Remember to add some veggies onto the plate.

When dinner is over, clean up first, and then serve dessert!

Day Seven

Vanilla Ice Cream with Raspberries and Chocolate Chips

Congratulations! You did it! A whole week of healthy recipes are good for them, and good for you!

GOOD JOB!

Note: If you would like to know how to make substitutions to the recipes in this book, you can check out my website: www.janetlaidler.com. I am working on a second book another week's worth of recipes which should be out soon.

Recipes

Tartar Sauce

Prep time less than 5 minutes

Ingredients	Tools
1/2 cup mayonnaise **one slice of onion (about ¼ inch thick)** **cream of tartar powder** **1 slice of dill pickle** **¼ teaspoon cumin** **small lime wedge**	**measuring spoons** **measuring cup** **cutting board** **small knife to cut pickle** **a spoon**

1) Put the mayonnaise, onion powder, cream of tartar to the measuring cup.
2) With the cutting board, slice the pickle slice and the onion slice, into small pieces.
3) Add these, and the cumin, and a squeeze of lime to the measuring cup and mix it with the spoon.
4) It is ready to serve.

Dad's Favorite Pot Roast

Start this 3 hours before dinner. Prep time: is about 25 minutes in total.

<u>Part 1</u> – preheat oven to 300 degrees

<u>Ingredients</u>	<u>Tools</u>
2 lb. chuck roast	large fork
1 tablespoon sweet paprika	comfortable knife to cut with
½ teaspoon onion powder	cutting board
salt & pepper	large stovetop pot with lid
dash of ground coffee	measuring cup
1 medium carrot	spatula
1 stalk celery	cooking tongs
1 medium brown onion	potato masher
¼ yellow bell pepper	blender
½ tsp. minced garlic	oven mitts
1 leaf collard green	large fork
1 kale leaf	serving dish or bowl to put
4 tablespoons olive oil	the meat into
¼ teaspoon flaxseed	large spoon
one bay leaf	blender
1 tablespoon olive oil	spatula
½ teaspoon salt	knife to slice meat
¼ teaspoon pepper	medium size pan
1 teaspoon sweet paprika	
1 teaspoon onion powder	
1 small russet potato	
3 to 4 cauliflower florets	
¼ cup water	
¼ of a lime	

1) Using the cutting board and the knife, cut and peel the brown skin from the onion and cut off the stem. Cut the onion into 4 pieces.
2) Do the same to the carrot, celery, pepper, kale and collards.
3) Place the meat on the cutting board and spear it with the large fork to hold it in place. Cut the roast in 3 to 4 pieces.
4) Place the pot on the stove, add 2 tbsp. olive oil, and the paprika, onion powder, salt and pepper, turn on to medium heat and let the pan get hot.
5) Using the large fork put the roast pieces into the pan; quickly searing and browning all sides. This should take no more than a minute on each side.

6) Once browned, add about 2 tablespoons of water and stir the juices in the pan. Then add all of the vegetable that you just cut, plus the flaxseed. Stir the vegetables up and around the meat.
7) Put the lid on and place into a preheated oven for 2 hours.

Part 2: About 30 minutes before dinner

8) Peel the potato. Cut the potato and the cauliflower florets into about 2 inch chunks.
9) Place them in the medium pan and cover with water. Add a dash of salt.
10) Bring to a boil and cook for about 20 minutes, or until they are soft enough to insert a fork.
11) While this is boiling, and using your oven mitts, take the roast out of the oven and let it sit.
12) Once done put oven mitts on and drain the water.
13) Using the masher, mash the cauliflower and potatoes together until smooth.
14) Next, remove the lid from the pan and with your tongs, remove the bay leaf and throw it away.
15) Next, remove the meat and place it on a plate. Put the pot lid over the meat to keep it warm.
16) Get your blender and pour/scrape all the remaining ingredients into the blender.
17) Put the lid on the blender, and turn the blender on mix for about 20 seconds, then turn it up for a few more seconds so the mixture forms a puree. For the final touch, add the squeeze of lime juice and blend for about 5 more seconds.
18) Scoop some of the potato mixture onto the plate and put some pieces of the meat next to it. You may slice it if you like. Then pour the gravy over both.
19) You are ready to eat!

Basic Olive Oil Salad Dressing

Prep time: approximately 5 minutes   Servings: 8 - 12

Ingredients	Tools
2 tablespoons white wine vinegar ¼ teaspoon onion powder ¼ teaspoon sugar 3/4 cup olive oil 1 tablespoon water 1/8 teaspoon salt 1/8 teaspoon finely ground pepper	measuring cup Small fork measuring spoons 16 oz. container (I recommend a glass jar with a secure lid so you can shake it before using.)

1) Using your measuring spoons, add the vinegar, onion powder and sugar into one of the measuring cups.
2) Whisk with the fork until the sugar and onion powder are dissolved.
3) Add the olive oil and water.
4) Mixture should equal exactly one cup.
5) Whisk with the fork until creamy.
6) Use what you need and put the rest in the container to store for future use.

Notes:

-You do not have to store this in the refrigerator as you will be using it on a regularly.

-If you do choose to refrigerate it, make sure you take it out to warm to room temperature at least 10 minutes before using it as the olive oil will solidify making it difficult to shake or blend it together

Italian Dressing

Simply repeat the above and add the following:

Ingredients
½ teaspoon Italian herbs ½ teaspoon minced garlic 1 tablespoon grated parmesan cheese

Oatmeal Cookies

Prep time about 10 minutes. Cooking time: 8 – 10 minutes a batch.

Ingredients	Tools
1 tablespoon flaxseed	*electric mixer
½ cup butter (room temperature)	large mixing bowl
2 tablespoon olive oil	rubber spatula
¾ cup brown sugar – packed	spoon
1 egg	2 measuring cup
1 teaspoon vanilla	measuring spoons
½ teaspoon baking soda	baking sheet
¼ teaspoon salt	oven mitts
1 1/4 cup oat four	optional: cooling rack
2 teaspoons cinnamon	
1 ¼ cup rolled oats	
1/4 cup raisins	
¼ cup dried cranberries	
Optional:	
¼ cup finely chopped nuts	
¼ cup semi-sweet chocolate chips	

Electric mixer is optional. You can mix it by hand and get great results.

1) Preheat oven to 325 degrees.
2) Put the flaxseed in a measuring cup, add 3 tablespoons of boiling water. Let it sit until the water is absorbed.
3) Add butter, sugar and one tablespoon of olive oil in a large mixing bowl. Mix on low speed until combined.
4) Add the egg and vanilla. Mix on low until blended.
5) Add the baking soda and salt and blend.
6) Add the flour and cinnamon. Mix on low speed.
7) Add the rolled oats and flaxseed and mix well.
8) Add the remaining desired ingredients and mix well on low speed.
9) Grease the baking sheet with the remaining olive oil.
10) Use a teaspoon to scoop dough onto prepared baking pan and place about an inch apart.
11) Bake for 8 - 10 minutes, or until slightly puffy and lightly golden brown on top. Cooking time may vary depending on size of the cookies.
12) With oven mitts on, take the cookies out of the oven and place pan on cooling rack (or any heat resistant cool surface) to cool for at least 5 minutes.

Banana Cupcakes

Prep time about 10 minutes. Cooking time: 20 minutes

<u>Ingredients</u>	<u>Tools</u>
1 tablespoon flaxseed	electric mixer
3 medium bananas	large mixing bowl
¼ cup (1/2 stick) butter	dinner fork
2/3 cup sugar	rubber spatula
3 eggs	2 measuring cup
1 ¾ cup flour	measuring spoons
½ teaspoon salt	cupcakes tin
1 teaspoon baking powder*	paper cupcake cups
1 teaspoon baking soda	a spoon or ice cream scoop
1 tablespoon apple cider vinegar	oven mitts
1/4 cup milk	Optional:
Optional:	cooling rack
2 teaspoons walnut extract	
or ½ cup finely chopped walnuts	
*use 2 teaspoons with gluten free flours	

1) Preheat oven to 350 degrees.
2) Put the flaxseed in a measuring cup and add 3 tablespoons of boiling water. Let it sit until the water is absorbed.
3) Put the bananas in the mixing bowl and mash with a fork until chunky, then mix them with the electric mixer until almost smooth.
4) Add the butter and sugar. Mix on medium speed until creamy.
5) Add the eggs. Mix on medium until blended.
6) Add the flour, salt, baking powder, baking soda and mix well.
7) Put the vinegar into the measuring cup with milk, and stir. Add to the cake mixture and blend.
8) Add the remaining ingredients as desired.
9) Place the cupcake paper cups into the cupcake tin and use the scoop to put even amounts of batter (approximately 1/8 inch from top of cup) into each one.
10) Place in preheated oven for about 20 minutes, or until slightly puffy and lightly golden brown on top.
11) With oven mitts on, pull the pan out of the oven and Insert a toothpick to check for doneness. If there is liquid batter on the toothpick, keep them in the oven for another minute or so. Do not overcook!
12) Let them cool for at least 20 minutes before adding frosting.

Buttercream Frosting
Prep time about 10 minutes.

Ingredients	Tools
1 cup unsalted butter	electric mixer
¼ cup sugar	2 mixing bowls
1 tablespoon whole milk	rubber spatula
1 teaspoon vanilla*	A measuring cup
1 egg white	measuring spoons
1 tablespoon lemon or lime zest*	small pan
can be substituted	mixing spoon

1) Put egg white into a bowl and beat with the electric mixer on highest speed until it is stiff, meaning the egg whites will form peaks. Set this aside.
2) Put the butter in the other mixing bowl and beat on medium high speed until creamy and smooth, almost fluffy.
3) Put the sugar and milk in the small pan on the stove on a low heat. Stir until the sugar is completely melted.
4) Once the sugar is melted, add it slowly to the butter with the mixer on low speed.
5) Once all of the sugar is mixed in, add the vanilla (or zest) and whip the butter on the highest speed until it becomes light, smooth and fluffy again.
6) With the spatula and two tablespoons at a time, fold the egg white into the butter.
7) If the buttercream is too soft, then refrigerate for ½ an hour and whip on high speed to fluff it up.
8) It should be ready to go.

References and Resources

1) Parkinson's Disease, 300 tips for making life easier, by Shelley Peterman Schwarz
2) Eating Well for Optimal Health, the essential guide to bringing health and pleasure back to eating, by Andrew Weil, M.D.
3) Parkinson's Disease, the complete guide for patients and caregiver, by Abraham N. Lieberman, M.D. and Frank L. Williams, Executive Director, American Parkinson's Disease Association
4) What Your doctor May Not Tell You About Parkinson's Disease, a Holistic program for optimal wellness, by Jill Marjama-Lyons, M.D. and Mary J. Shomon
5) Herbal Remedies, a reference guide, Andrew Chevallier
6) Eating for Your Brain as a Senior, by Lisa Esposito, US News and World Report, January 5, 2016
7) Institute on Aging, Non-profit Senior Help and Care, www.IOAging.org
8) National Institute on Aging, A Leader in Aging Research, https://www.nia.nih.gov
9) The Mind Diet, A diet formulated to include phytonutrients proven to reduce and reverse the effects of Alzheimer's Disease on the Brain, A study published at Rush University, developed by Martha Claire Morris, Phd.
10) The Mediterranean Diet, developed by the Mayo Clinic
11) The Dash Diet, by Marla Heller
12) Dr. Robert Milne, Las Vegas, NV
13) Dr. Christopher Whitty, Riverview, MI

Made in the USA
Lexington, KY
22 December 2016